OLD NUBIAN MIRACLE OF ST. MENA

Translated by: Francis Llewellyn Griffith
Introduction by: D.P. Curtin

Dalcassian
Publishing
Company

PHILADELPHIA, PA

ISBN: 978-1-960069-67-2 (Paperback)

Library of Congress Control Number:
Author: Curtin, D.P. (1985-)

Front cover image: Sandstone frieze, early 7th century, from Faras (Nubia), Republic of Sudan, British Museum
Book design by J.J. Ripplestick

Printed by Ingram Content Group, 1 Ingram Blvd, La Vergne, Tennessee

First printing edition 2021.

INTRODUCTION

Within the broader orthodox communion, there is the relatively well-known split between the Eastern and Oriental Orthodox churches. Eastern Orthodoxy maintains a litany of familiar churches, of both the autonomous and autocephalous nature, with names of ethnicities that are not unfamiliar to most Christians today. Certainly, the fame of the Greek St. Nicolaus or St. George are well known even at the extreme distance of the boundaries of their homeland. Much the same, St. Francis amongst the Latins or St. Anthony amongst the Egyptians are regarded well beyond the limits of their own specific faith tradition.

However, in all of this, there are elements of the Christian church that have become entirely forgotten. Today, the various St. Thomas Christians of India regret the loss of their earliest traditions, damaged by the coming of the Portuguese in the 16th century. Or, by the same token, the ancient Persian church was damaged by a progressive wave of conquerors who took hold of the region in succession. However, perhaps the most forgotten apostolic Christianity is that of Nubia, which rose in the 6th century and flourished for a thousand years before its disappearance. Precious little remains of this ancient church. Some of its time-beaten cathedrals have become a curiosity to archaeologists and art historians. However, the remnants of that community appear to have been shattered by the collapse of the three medieval kingdoms which held the torch of the Christian church in the face of so many external political pressures.

There are no Nubian hagiographies, no Nubian synaxarium of saints. It may be contested whether this ever existed, as a point of scholarship. However, the books and history of the Nubian church only survive as passing fragments. The Nubian church represents a lost Christianity, one that was heavily informed and related to its parent church, the Coptic Orthodox Church in Alexandria, as well as the Ethiopian Tewahedo Church in Axum to the south.

This work recalls the comical miracle of a Coptic saint, which was composed around the 10th century in the Old Nubian language. It represents the most complete hagiography that has survived from the Nubian church. Its subject was the 4th century Egyptian martyr, Mena of Phrygia, commonly called a soldier in the Roman Army. He remains a popular saint in the Egyptian church, and apparently was something akin to a national saint prior to the Arab invasion. A cathedral was named for him in Egypt which stood in what is now Abu Mena in the Western Desert. Its destruction under the Rashidun Caliphate is perhaps symbolic of the end of Coptic cultural autonomy.

Little is known regarding the veneration of St. Mena in Nubia. An illustration relating to this tale has been found, depicting the saint with his three crowns of martyrdom. The inscription grants him name in a linguistically ambiguous way, as it reads the same in Greek, Coptic, and Old Nubian.

Therefore, this text represents a rare and unparalleled window into the life of the Nubian church. It grants details that are not found elsewhere in either Coptic or Ethiopian sources, and perhaps gives a sense of the dry humor that may have been present in the life of the community as they sought to comprehend the great mystery of the life of St. Mena and his eventual martyrdom.

D. P. Curtin
Glen Mills, PA
Jan. 1, 2021

The miracle which the martyr (ⲘⲀⲢⲦⲨⲢ) of Christ (ⲬⲢⲒⲤⲦⲞⲤ), Saint Mena performed. In the peace of God, Amen.

Beloved: a certain woman was dwelling in a certain village in the suburbs of Alexandria (Alexandria). And she was sterile and having wedded did not bear, neither son nor daughter; and she possessed much wealth in [...] and had not an heir. And she spoke concerning this thing and took shame in her heart. And moreover, all dwelling in her house were sterile, girls of service [and] cattle down to fowls. And on one among the days, that woman heard the monks of the Christians (ϮⲎⲢⲒⲤⲦⲒⲀⲚⲞⲤ) telling the wonders which Saint Mena was doing in the church of Mareotis (ⲚⲀⲢⲈⲞⲦⲒⲤ), and she then said "Verily, if the God of Saint Mena commanded one amongst my fowls to lay [an egg], [so] I also will deposit the egg that it hath first laid in his church."

When much time had been accomplished, one in the fowls conceived and laid one egg. And that woman took the egg and came down to the water with one servant-girl, [so] that she might find a boat and take that egg unto the church of Saint Mena situated in Mareotis.

And having found a boat about to go to Philoxenite (ⲠⲎⲒⲖⲟⲜⲉⲚⲓⲦⲉ) and loaded [...], the woman said to the sailor "Rejoice, my father the sailor!", and he said, "Rejoice also thou!" And the woman said, Verily, this [...] having made ready [...] whether will it go?"

The boatman replied "Verily, if the Lord [shall] preserve me, I shall go to Philoxenite."

And the woman said "If thou wilt endure [...], do a favor [...] with me and convey me [...] with thee to Philoxenite.

The boatman replied "What wouldest thou there?"

The woman replied, "I will go to the church of Saint Mena."
And the boatman said, "But thou being [...] pagan (ⲈⲖⲖⲎⲚ) what wilt thou do in the church?"

The woman replied "I shall dedicate this egg in that church, that the god of Saint Mena may give me seed of conception [...]. Verily, if I am about to [...] bear, I'll become a Christian" (ⲬⲠⲒⲤⲦⲒⲀⲚⲞⲤ).

The boatman replied, "O woman, but thou art tender [...], and not loving hardship [...], and give me thine egg which I will deposit and do thou return to thy house that thy husband may not fear."

And the woman believed (pisteyein) and put the egg in his hand. And she returned to her house with her service-girl. And the boatman took the egg, carried it into the hold [...] and laid it in the [...], until [his] coming to Philoxenite. And when many days had passed, he came to the shore of Philoxenite. And the man forgot the egg and behold [...] returned to the other [...] extremity [...]. And on one in the days, the boatman saw that egg that it was in the [...] of the hold [...] of the boat, namely this which he had laid down and forgotten.

He said to his son "Boy, whence was this egg?"

And he said, "My father, dost thou not remember this, which a woman gave us that [...] we might put them in the church of Saint Mena?"

And the father said to the hoy "O, it is [...] true. Cook it that I may have food."

And his son cooked and brought [...] it and sent food. And when the days of three new moons had passed, they came to a village, and they moved up the boat to the bank of that village. And when it was Sunday (ⲕⲩⲡⲓⲁⲕⲏ) the boatman came up to the village that he might receive the sacrament. And in that village, there was set the church of the Holy Virgin (Parthenos) Mary, and he entered therein [...] to take the sacrament. And after [...] the Trisagion (ⲧⲡⲓⲥⲁⲅⲓⲟⲛ) had been sung [...], and [...] all the people gathered [...] to the font [...], that they might write [...] the water [...] of the holy one (agios) and the eye of the boatman was opened and saw in the mirror [...] Saint Mena coming mounted on a white horse, and aiming [...] at him a spear of flame [...]. And having seen [this], he rushed and came to the image (eikon) of Mary bearer of God, cried and said, "By thy power [...] Mary bearer of God, save me, for [...] I have committed sin."

And Saint Mena standing again [...] said to him "What shall I do with thee on the day of to-day? Is it by the power [...] of my mistress that thou hast [...] gone forth?"

And when [...] the Saint seized that man and trampled [...] him upon the head, the egg, which he had eaten immediately [...] became a live fowl, descended verily under him, came out. stood up and instantly [...] crowed. And Saint Mena, seated on the horse took the fowl by its two wings, carried it and said "Go [...] hither [...] be [...] after this."

And Saint Mena went forth to the house of that woman knocked [...] at the door and called [...], and that woman running [...] came' and opened the door.
And the Saint said to her "Woman, receive this fowl and let it out amongst thy fowls that they may make thee fruitful. And thou also O woman, the son that thou shalt bear, call his name Mena. Likewise, also thy girls of service shall be fruitful and thy cattle. And do thou, O woman, receive baptism for the remission of thy sins"

[...] and having finished [...] saying this, immediately [...] the Saint vanished [...]. And the woman having taken the fowl and put it out with her fowls, immediately [...] thus [...] they became fruitful, [and] the girls of service and the cattle. And she the woman moreover conceived and bore a boy-baby and called his name Mena as the Saint had said to her. And her girls of service also conceived likewise and brought forth son and daughter. And that woman, when the days of her solitude were completed, came out to the church of Saint Mena, to Mareotis. And when she came into the holy church, she asked for [...] the priest [...] that he might baptize them. And the priest took them, and prayed for them, and baptized her and her husband and her son and her servants in the name of the Father and the Son and the Holy Ghost. And thus, being converted as Christians they remained every day of their life and lived as members [...] of the church of Saint Mena offering their first fruits [...] to the church, until their death. And all having seen and heard of this great miracle glorified God and Saint Mena. Whose is the glory and the power, now and in all time" unto the eternity of ages. Amen (ⲀⲘⲎⲚ).

The Scriptorium Project is the work of a small group of lay people of various apostolic churches who are interested in the preservation, transmission, and translation of the works of the early and medieval church. Our efforts are to make the works of the church fathers accessible to anyone who might have an interest in Christian antiquities and the theological, philosophical, and moral writings that have become the bedrock of Western Civilization.

To-date, our releases have pulled from the Greek, Syriac, Georgian, Latin, Celtic, Ethiopian, and Coptic traditions of Christianity, and have been pulled from sundry local traditions and languages.

Other Titles and Translations by D.P. Curtin:

First Book of Ethiopian Maccabees (2018)
Protoevangelium of James: Greek and English Texts (2019)
Edicts of the Synod of Paris by Chlothar II, King of Franks (2019)
The Life of St. Desiderius by Sisebut, King of Visigoths (2019)
The Synod of Rome by St. Boniface IV of Rome (2019)
Letter to Pope Theodore by Victor of Carthage (2020)
The Decree of 610 by Gundemar, King of Visigoths (2020)
Laws of the Church by Dagobert I, King of Franks (2020)
The Old Nubian Miracle of St. Mena (2021)
About Fifteen Problems by St. Albertus Magnus (2022)
Testament of Some Former Things by John Scotus Eriugena (2022)
The Georgian Synaxarium (2022)
Instructions: Counsel for Novices by St. Ammonas the Hermit (2022)
The Syriac Menologium and Martyrology (2022)
Book on Religious Exercise and Quiet by St. Isaiah the Solitary (2022)
Vision of Theophilus by St. Cyril of Alexandria (2022)
On Fate (De Fato) by St. Albertus Magnus (2023)
Fragments of 'Chronicle' by Hippolytus of Thebes (2023)
Life of the Blessed Theotokos by Epiphanius Monachus (2023)
Syriac Life of John the Baptist by Serapion the Presbyter (2023)
Second Book of Ethiopian Maccabees (2023)

www.ingramcontent.com/pod-product-compliance
Lightning Source LLC
Chambersburg PA
CBHW070959120626
46546CB00004B/1693